IMPROVING PARENT-ADOLESCENT RELATIONSHIPS

LEARNING ACTIVITIES FOR PARENTS AND ADOLESCENTS

PARTICIPANT WORKBOOK

DARRELL J. BURNETT, PH.D.

Accelerated Development
A member of the Taylor & Francis Group

IMPROVING PARENT-ADOLESCENT RELATIONSHIPS
Learning Activities for Parents and Adolescents
Participant Workbook

Technical Development: Tanya Benn
Delores Kellogg
Cynthia Long
Marguerite Mader
Sheila Sheward

ISBN: 1-55959-035-1

Order additional copies from

Accelerated Development
A member of the Taylor & Francis Group
47 Runway Road, Suite G
Levittown, PA 19057-4700
1-800-821-8312

3/05

DEDICATION

To my loving wife, Susann,
for her inspiration, encouragement,
typing, and proofreading.
To my wonderful children, Matt, Tom, and Jill,
for their humor, energy, and support.

PREFACE

When I began to develop and gather materials for this program, I was looking for an end product that would be **practical, inexpensive, relevant,** and **applicable** in a wide variety of settings.

The topics covered in this program evolved over a four year period during which I was leading multifamily groups for parents and adolescents in inpatient settings, outpatient clinics, and occasionally for juvenile court diversion programs. Through feedback from parents and adolescents as to which **topics** they felt were most relevant, and which **activities** they felt were most productive. The program eventually evolved into 15 sessions covering three main topic areas: (1) perceiving each other (social perception), (2) communicating effectively, and (3) recognizing behavior as a function of its consequence. The enthusiastic response of participants emphasized these three areas.

The activities involving social perception in the first three sessions received remarks such as the following:

> "It's about time I'm getting my parent to look at the way **I** see things!"

> "I never thought I'd see the day my **kid** would actually try to look at how I see things!"

The effective communication activities received responses such as the following:

> "Thanks to the structured activities, the prepared scripts, and the scoring grid, we were able to stay 'on track'!"

> "I liked being able to talk to my parents about negative feelings without all the yelling and screaming that usually goes on."

> "The activities really help us talk in a civil manner to each other on touchy subjects."

> "I've never tried to 'get into my parent's shoes' before. What a trip!"

> "When we did those empathy activities, I couldn't believe it. There we were, actually focusing on each others' thoughts and feelings without getting defensive. A parent's dream! A major breakthrough for us!"

The activities that centered around recognizing behavior as a function of its consequence were extremely well received, with statements such as the following:

> "It's great to be able to work on skills, learning to **do** something about our complaints with each other instead of mutual finger pointing."

> "I like the 'no fault' approach to problem solving. We used our energy solving instead of blaming."

> "The contract activity was something else! I never thought I'd be able to actually sit down and **negotiate** with my parents!"

Besides the topics which evolved, the **approach** used in the program was also determined by the response of the participants. They seemed to prefer the **structured, hands-on, skills training** approach rather than a generalized, unstructured discussion group. Some of their responses were the following:

> "The structured activities made the sessions more productive. No one family was able to monopolize the sessions. We all had a chance to learn the materials."

> "I like the emphasis on learning **skills** rather than airing our dirty laundry in front of everybody."

The fact that the program involves parents and adolescents participating **together** in each session was a positive feature mentioned repeatedly.

> "We didn't have to 'role play' what we **would** say to our parents if they were there. They **were** there! And we got to practice face-to-face with them!"

> "Just having our son in the same room practicing the activities with us, made the whole program seem more like a 'family' activity, not an 'us vs. him' situation."

Although the program developed in the context of a multifamily group, the materials and sessions work equally well for individual family treatment.

Finally, just as this program evolved over time, it may well continue to develop. Accordingly, if, in the process of using these materials, new applications arise, I would appreciate feedback of ideas for future additions or revisions.

Darrell J. Burnett, Ph.D.

CONTENTS

LIST OF FORMS

INTRODUCTION

PURPOSE OF THE PROGRAM

The purpose of the parent-adolescent relationship program is to offer a learning experience for parents and adolescents working together to improve their skills in the areas which are the foundation for healthy family living: 1) *perceiving each other;* 2) *communicating effectively,* and 3) *recognizing behavior as a function of its consequences.* The sessions are organized under three major parts.

Perceiving Each Other

The first three sessions dwell on the practical and pertinent topic of social perception, how people view other people. These sessions address the age old "generation gap" experience, helping parents and adolescents to see "eye to eye." These sessions will offer you an opportunity to become aware of how *close* or how *far away* you are from each other in the way you perceive each other's *personality* (Session 1), in the way you perceive how *communications* are going within your family (Session 2), and the way you perceive each other's *values* (Session 3).

Hopefully, through these social perception activities, you will learn the skills of accurate perception of each other, acknowledging similarities and differences.

Communicating Effectively

The next six sessions dwell on the topic of **communication,** exposing you to the various styles of communication between parents and adolescents. The sessions will help you identify and develop assertive problem-solving approaches to communications within the family. The various topics include **styles** of communication (Session 4); distinguishing among **assertive, aggressive,** and **passive** problem-solving approaches (Session 5); effective communication **techniques** while expressing **feelings** concerning family topics (Session 6); **positive** feelings toward family members (Session 7); **negative** feelings toward family members (Session 8); and feelings of **empathy** toward family members (Session 9).

The purpose of these sessions is to help you improve your skill at "getting your point across" while standing up for yourself, yet recognizing the dignity and point of view of the other family member(s).

Recognizing Behavior as a Function of Its Consequences

The final six sessions dwell on the general topic of understanding **why** behaviors occur, and learning some **techniques** for changing or managing the behaviors of family members within the home setting. Topics for the sessions include: **The Law Effect:** understanding how consequences play a major role in influencing behaviors (Session 10); **theories** of **why adolescents do what they do** (Session 11); the **role** which **parents** play in **applying consequences** for behaviors at home (Session 12); **assessing** how **negative consequences** are **applied** at home, distinguishing between **punishment** and **logical and natural consequences** (Session 13); learning to **identify** and spell out **behaviors** with family members (Session 14); and setting up a **family behavior contract** (Session 15).

STRUCTURE

The program is set up as a series of 15 **skills training sessions.** Each session involves a specific topic with hands-on paper-pencil activities, active participation, and occasional lectures.

Each participant receives a *Workbook* containing most of the forms used in the workshop. The emphasis is upon **teaching problem-solving skills** rather than having family members sitting around blaming each other.

The program is **positive** in its approach. It's not a forum for "airing dirty family laundry" in front of others.

Each session is **self-contained,** but many follow logically from the previous session.

LENGTH OF WORKSHOP

Each of the 15 sessions lasts approximately 50 to 60 minutes.

Part I

PERCEIVING
EACH OTHER

PERSONALITY TRAITS

In this session you will have an opportunity to better understand how you "see" one another in terms of your *personality traits.*

You will have an opportunity to recognize how **close** or how *far away* you are from each other in the way you describe each other (parents describing adolescents and vice versa).

The paper and pencil activities will give you the chance to practice social perception exercises with family members and learn the importance of *accurate social perception* in family communications.

NOTES
Related to Session 1
(Add Your Notes)

SOCIAL PERCEPTION

ITS EFFECT ON
FAMILY COMMUNICATION

When family members communicate with each other, their **behavior communicates how they see themselves,** but, more important, it communicates how they see the **others.** For example, if family members perceive another family member as an unworthy person, their behavior toward that family member may communicate rejection. Self-perception and the perception of others become central in understanding family communication in general, and communication in maltreating families in particular.

A person's behavior at any given moment is influenced by that person's current perceptions of self and other and by previously acquired and reinforced patterns of communication with the other person. Thus, in order to understand a family's interaction patterns, we need to understand how the family members view themselves and each other. We also need to understand how the perception of self and others interacts with previously developed patterns of communication and with general personal characteristics of the family members to create altogether unique patterns of interaction and mutual behaviors.

Form 1. Family Social Perception: Parent Form

DIRECTIONS

1. As a parent, complete this form.
2. Use current descriptions and/or current behavioral examples.

Part A: How I describe myself.

1. _____   6. _____
2. _____   7. _____
3. _____   8. _____
4. _____   9. _____
5. _____   10. _____

Part B: How I describe my teenager.

1. _____   6. _____
2. _____   7. _____
3. _____   8. _____
4. _____   9. _____
5. _____   10. _____

Part C: How my teenager describes me.

1. _____   6. _____
2. _____   7. _____
3. _____   8. _____
4. _____   9. _____
5. _____   10. _____

(Continued)

Form 1 Continued

Part D: What my teenager looks for in picking friends.

1. _____
2. _____
3. _____
4. _____
5. _____

6. _____
7. _____
8. _____
9. _____
10. _____

Part E: What I look for in my teenager's friends.

1. _____
2. _____
3. _____
4. _____
5. _____

6. _____
7. _____
8. _____
9. _____
10. _____

Part F: My teenager's friends whom I like and why.

Name

Why

_____   _____

_____   _____

_____   _____

_____   _____

Form 2. Family Social Perception: Adolescent Form

DIRECTIONS

1. As an adolescent and member of the family, complete this form.
2. Use current descriptions and/or behavioral examples.

Part A: How I describe myself.

1. _____
2. _____
3. _____
4. _____
5. _____

6. _____
7. _____
8. _____
9. _____
10. _____

Part B: How I describe my parents.

1. _____
2. _____
3. _____
4. _____
5. _____

6. _____
7. _____
8. _____
9. _____
10. _____

Part C: How my parents describe me.

1. _____
2. _____
3. _____
4. _____
5. _____

6. _____
7. _____
8. _____
9. _____
10. _____

(Continued)

Form 2 Continued

Part D: What my parents want me to look for in picking my friends.

1. _____   6. _____

2. _____   7. _____

3. _____   8. _____

4. _____   9. _____

5. _____   10. _____

Part E: What I look for in picking my friends.

1. _____   6. _____

2. _____   7. _____

3. _____   8. _____

4. _____   9. _____

5. _____   10. _____

Part F: Friends whom my parents like, and why.

Name   Why

_____   _____

_____   _____

_____   _____

COMMUNICATING WITHIN THE FAMILY

This session continues to emphasize social perception, but this time, instead of discussing personality traits, you will have a chance to discuss how you **communicate** with each other.

Parents, you will be able to compare your view of yourself as a communicator in the family with your **adolescent's view** of you as a communicator.

Adolescents, you will have the chance to compare notes with your **parents** on specific items of the family communication questionnaire. Please answer **honestly** and be sure to base your answers on **current** behaviors.

This session is another opportunity to see how close or how far away you are from each other (parents and adolescents) in the way you see the **patterns** of **family communication.**

NOTES
Related to Session 2

Form 3. Communication Questionnaire For The Parents*

DIRECTIONS

1. Read each question carefully.
2. Circle the number which best describes your true feelings.
3. Be honest in each of your responses.
4. Base your answers on current behaviors (past six months).

	Never	Almost Never	Some-times	Almost Always	Always
1. Are you interested in the things your adolescent does and is interested in?	1	2	3	4	5
2. Do you stick to the subject when you talk to your adolescent?	1	2	3	4	5
3. Is your adolescent able to say what he/she feels around home?	1	2	3	4	5
4. Do you interrupt your adolescent before he/she has finished talking?	1	2	3	4	5
5. Do you talk to your adolescent as if he/she were younger than he/she is?	1	2	3	4	5
6. Do you find yourself thinking about other things while you are talking with your adolescent?	1	2	3	4	5
7. Does your family talk things over with each other?	1	2	3	4	5
8. Does your adolescent disagree with your opinions?	1	2	3	4	5
9. Do you listen to and value your adolescent's opinion?	1	2	3	4	5
10. Do you make clear the things you mean to say?	1	2	3	4	5
11. When your adolescent has personal problems, does he/she discuss them with you?	1	2	3	4	5
12. Do you ask to hear your adolescent's side of things?	1	2	3	4	5

(Continued)

*Adapted by Darrell J. Burnett, Ph.D., with permission from Brownstone, J.E., & Dye, C.J. (1973). *Communication Workshop for Parents of Adolescents: Leader's Guide.* Champaign, IL: Research Press.

Form 3 Continued

	Never	Almost Never	Some-times	Almost Always	Always
13. Do you discuss matters of sex with your adolescent?	1	2	3	4	5
14. Are there times when you feel your adolescent can't do anything right?	1	2	3	4	5
15. Do you trust your adolescent?	1	2	3	4	5
16. Do you have confidence in your adolescent's abilities?	1	2	3	4	5
17. Do you usually stay calm when you talk about a problem?	1	2	3	4	5
18. Do you explain your reasons for objecting to something your adolescent wants to do?	1	2	3	4	5
19. Do you feel that you and your adolescent seldom talk except when someone is upset or angry?	1	2	3	4	5
20. Do you find your adolescent "tuning you out" instead of talking with you?	1	2	3	4	5
21. Do you feel your adolescent shows respect for your ideas and opinions?	1	2	3	4	5
22. Do you wish that you and your adolescent could communicate better?	1	2	3	4	5

Now complete these statements:

23. When I think about the future, I worry most about _____

_____

24. The best thing about our family is _____

25. I would like to be able to talk to my adolescent about _____

_____

26. Most adolescents don't realize that _____

_____

Form 4. Communication Questionnaire For The Adolescent*

DIRECTIONS

1. Read each question carefully.
2. Circle the number which best describes your true feelings.
3. Be honest in each of your responses.
4. Base your answers on current behaviors (past six months).

	Never	Almost Never	Some-times	Almost Always	Always
1. Do your parents seem interested in the things you do and are interested in?	1	2	3	4	5
2. When your parents sit down and talk to you about a specific problem, do they bring in a lot of other issues by the time they're through?	1	2	3	4	5
3. Are you able to say what you really feel around home?	1	2	3	4	5
4. Do your parents keep you from finishing what you have to say to them by interrupting?	1	2	3	4	5
5. Do your parents tend to talk to you as if you were much younger than you actually are?	1	2	3	4	5
6. Do your parents seem to be thinking about other things while you're trying to talk to them?	1	2	3	4	5
7. Does your family talk things over with each other?	1	2	3	4	5
8. Do you hesitate to disagree with either of your parents? Which one? _____ Both? _____	1	2	3	4	5
9. Do your parents listen to and value your opinion?	1	2	3	4	5
10. Are you sometimes confused about what your parents really mean by what they say?	1	2	3	4	5

(Continued)

*Adapted by Darrell J. Burnett, Ph.D., with permission from Brownstone, J.E., & Dye, C.J. (1973). *Communication Workshop for Parents of Adolescents: Leader's Guide.* Champaign, IL: Research Press

Form 4 Continued

	Never	Almost Never	Some-times	Almost Always	Always
11. When you have personal problems, do you discuss them with your parents?	1	2	3	4	5
12. Do your parents ask to hear your side of things?	1	2	3	4	5
13. Are you able to discuss matters of sex with your parents? Which one? _____ Both? _____	1	2	3	4	5
14. Are there times when you feel your parents think you can't do anything right?	1	2	3	4	5
15. Do you feel that your parents trust you?	1	2	3	4	5
16. Do your parents have confidence in your abilities?	1	2	3	4	5
17. Do your parents often become upset when they talk to you about some problem?	1	2	3	4	5
18. Do your parents let you know their reasons for objecting to something you want to do?	1	2	3	4	5
19. Do you feel that you and your parents seldom talk except when someone is upset or angry?	1	2	3	4	5
20. Do you find yourself "tuning out" your parents instead of talking with them?	1	2	3	4	5
21. Do you feel that you show respect for your parents' ideas and opinions?	1	2	3	4	5
22. Do you wish that you and your parents could communicate better?	1	2	3	4	5

Now complete these statements:

23. When I think about the future, I worry most about _____

24. The best thing about our family is _____

25. I would like to be able to talk to my parents about _____

26. Most parents don't realize that _____

VALUES

In this session, continuing with the social perception activities, you will have a chance to compare and see how well you know each other's *values.*

The traditional *"generation gap"* has been a topic of discussion between adolescents and parents since recorded history. In this session you will have the opportunity to discuss the specifics of some of your own *values,* and *how* you *show* your *values* to each other.

NOTES
Related to Session 3

Form 5. Values: Parent Questionnaire*

Part A: Values

DIRECTIONS

1. Rank the values shown below in terms of their *importance* to you.
2. Rank from most important (1) to least important (10.) Each value must have a *separate* ranking. Thus, (1) is most important, (2) is second most important, etc.

_____	Equality	_____	Loyalty
_____	Family Life	_____	National Security
_____	Freedom of Individual Expression	_____	Peace
_____	Happiness	_____	Recognition of Other
_____	Leisure and the Arts	_____	Salvation

Which of these values will your parents rank as the three most important?

1. _____

2. _____

3. _____

Part B: Personality Traits

Directions:

1. Rank the personality traits shown below in terms of their *importance* to you.
2. Rank from most important (1) to least important (8). Each trait must have a *separate* ranking.

_____	Caring	_____	Productive
_____	Creative	_____	Responsible
_____	Open to Change	_____	Self-Confident
_____	Optimistic	_____	Truthful

Which of these personality traits will your parents rank as the three most important?

1. _____

2. _____

3. _____

*Adapted by Darrell J. Burnett, Ph.D., with permission from Brownstone, J.E., & Dye, C.J. (1973). *Communication Workshop for Parents of Adolescents: Leader's Guide.* Champaign, IL: Research Press.

Form 6. Values: Adolescent Questionnaire*

Part A: Values

DIRECTIONS

1. Rank the values shown below in terms of their **importance** to you.
2. Rank from most important (1) to least important (10.) Each value must have a **separate** ranking. Thus, (1) is most important, (2) is second most important, etc.

_____ Equality   _____ Loyalty

_____ Family Life   _____ National Security

_____ Freedom of Individual Expression   _____ Peace

_____ Happiness   _____ Recognition of Other

_____ Leisure and the Arts   _____ Salvation

Which of these values will your parents rank as the three most important?

Mom: 1. _____   Dad: 1. _____

2. _____   2. _____

3. _____   3. _____

Part B: Personality Traits

DIRECTIONS

1. Rank the personality traits shown below in terms of their **importance** to you.
2. Rank from most important (1) to least important (8). Each value must have a **separate** ranking.

_____ Caring   _____ Productive

_____ Creative   _____ Responsible

_____ Open to Change   _____ Self-Confident

_____ Optimistic   _____ Truthful

Which of these personality traits will your parents rank as the three most important?

Mom: 1. _____   Dad: 1. _____

2. _____   2. _____

3. _____   3. _____

*Adapted by Darrell J. Burnett, Ph.D., with permission from Brownstone, J.E., & Dye, C.J. (1973). *Communication Workshop for Parents of Adolescents: Leader's Guide*. Champaign, IL: Research Press.

Part II

COMMUNICATING

EFFECTIVELY

COMMUNICATION STYLES

Starting with this session, you will have an opportunity to begin to *develop* some healthy *communication patterns* within the family.

This session allows you to listen to four different *styles* of communication between *parents* and their *adolescents.*

As you listen to and discuss each style, think about which style is most common in your family.

Remember, *awareness* of the various styles of communication is the first step toward improving communications.

NOTES
Related to Session 4

Form 7. Parent-Adolescent Communication Styles: Answer Sheet

DIRECTIONS

1. One copy is to be completed by each family as a unit.
2. Answer all four questions for each style.
3. After completing Direction 2, you will be given Figure 1 to assist in your discussion.

RESPONSES TO STYLES

1. What name would you give to each style?

   Style A. _____

   Style B. _____

   Style C. _____

   Style D. _____

2. What are the weaknesses or strengths?

   Style A. _____

   Style B. _____

   Style C. _____

   Style D. _____

3. What was accomplished?

   Style A. _____

   Style B. _____

   Style C. _____

   Style D. _____

4. What are the feelings in the script of the parent and the adolescent?

   Style A. Mom _____

             Son _____

   Style B. Mom _____

             Son _____

   Style C. Dad _____

             Daughter _____

   Style D. Mom _____

             Son _____

Parent-Adolescent Communication Styles
Scripts*

Style A

Mom:	Steve, will you come in here?
Son:	Yes, Mom.
Mom:	I should have said you *will* come in here! Do you know what I want to talk to you about?
Son:	What?
Mom:	You tell me!
Son:	I'm late.
Mom:	Do you know what time it is?
Son:	Yes, Mother, I can read the clock.
Mom:	Don't get smart with me young man! Why weren't you here hours ago?
Son:	Do you want to know? Do you want to *listen* while I tell you?
Mom:	Yes, I'll listen. I want to know why you weren't here.
Son:	Well, we stopped for pizza after the game. They were real busy. It took us about an hour to get served. I couldn't get away. We were late.
Mom:	There you go with those same old excuses! You remember not 2 weeks ago your father and I sat down and told you to be home at 10:30 every night!
Son:	Here we go again.
Mom:	You just keep that up, young man, you just keep that up!
Son:	Now look, Mom, I'm not a kid any more!
Mom:	You're living in *my* house. You'll do what I want you to do! Now you're probably going to give me the silent treatment. You're probably going to go pout and shut up and not say anything.
Son:	Whatever!
Mom:	I want you to *listen* to me. When your father and I tell you to do something it's like you never hear a word we say! I'll bet right now you're not hearing a single word I say!
Son:	I hear every word you say, Mother, every time you say it!
Mom:	You just keep it up, young man, you just keep it up!
Son:	Aw Mom.
Mom:	Look, you can either follow the rules in our house, or you can leave!
Son:	I will leave, just as soon as I'm old enough to get out of here.
Mom:	You can leave right now! I'll help you pack!
Son:	I wish I *could* leave!
Mom:	Well I guess that means you're going to stay. That means you'll do what I tell you to do. And, to help you *learn* to do that, you're not going out for two weeks.
Son:	Oh c'mon I wasn't doing anything bad, we couldn't get home any earlier.
Mom:	You just keep that up and it'll be three weeks.
Son:	Aw c'mon!
Mom:	Alright, it's three weeks! And while you're staying in these three weeks maybe you'll think about being obedient to the rules your father and I set up.

---

*Adapted by Darrell J. Burnett, Ph.D., with permission from Brownstone, J.E., and Dye, C.J. (1973). *Communication workshop for parents and adolescents: Leader's guide.* Champaign, IL: Research Press.

Mom: Steve, I've been calling you and I'm not going to call you again.

Son: I just got a new tape and I wanted to listen to it on the big stereo in the family room.

Mom: Steve! Please come in here!

Son: OK, what do you want?

Mom: What do I want? You stand there with that look on your face and ask what do I want? What do you mean, what do I want?

Son: I don't know what you *want*. I've just been in the other room listening to a tape, and I have no way of knowing what you want!

Mom: Look around you. Look at your room. What's going on. What do you mean by this?

Son: What's wrong? Everything looks OK to me.

Mom: I can't believe it. I just don't know what I'm going to do with you. Now look, I bent over backwards for you. I told you if you didn't get this room cleaned up that you weren't going to that dance last Friday night at school. Then I gave in to you when you promised you'd clean it up the next day. You went to the dance, and you haven't even touched your room since then.

Son: Aw, Mom, hassle, hassle, hassle! That's all you do. You hassle me all the time! Besides the room's not that bad. And it's my room!

Mom: Well I just don't know what I'm going to do with you. Will you clean this up now, and I mean *now!* Or you're not going out the rest of the week. And I mean it!

Son: OK, OK, I'll do it in a minute.

Mom: Now, Steve. I want you to do it now!

Son: Mom, it's so silly to make such a big fuss over the room. I want to finish listening to my new tape now, just let me finish it, and then I'll do it. I promise.

Mom: Oh, just forget it. I'll do it myself. Just get out of here, and I'll do it myself.

Son: OK. Fine by me.

Style C

Dad:	Linda, will you come in here a minute before you go upstairs?
Daughter:	Sure Dad.
Dad:	I'd like to talk with you right now.
Daughter:	What about?
Dad:	Do you know what time it is, Linda?
Daughter:	I don't know, about 10:30 or 11?
Dad:	Check your watch again. It must be stopped!
Daughter:	Gee, I didn't know it was *that* late. I see what you mean. I guess it's pretty late.
Dad:	Honey, do you realize how much we worry about you when you don't get in on time?
Daughter:	I know you worry. But I was kind of in a bind tonight.
Dad:	We worry an awful lot, you know!
Daughter:	I would think you would trust me a little bit more than that, but I appreciate your worry.
Dad:	Linda, it's not that we don't trust you. Sure we trust you. But we don't trust everybody else. Remember when we showed you that newspaper clipping about that young girl and what happened to her when she was out late? We don't want that to happen to you.
Daughter:	I just didn't want to be the first to leave the group tonight. All the kids would have given me a hard time for going home so early and their parents don't seem to worry so much.
Dad:	Maybe other parents don't worry so much about their kids. But then maybe other parents don't care so much about their kids.
Daughter:	Yeah, I guess that's right.
Dad:	And another thing. Did you notice how the lights all went on down the block when you slammed the car door and said good night to whomever that was in the car? What do you think the neighbors are going to think about parents who don't get their daughter in at a decent hour? What are they going to think about you? What are they going to think about us?
Daughter:	Well, do you think maybe I could call you if it looked like I was going to be a little late?
Dad:	Yeah, maybe about 15 minutes or so. But we couldn't take much longer wondering if anything was happening to you and what you were doing. We just want you to start coming in a little earlier, because we hate not knowing where you are or what's going on. Right now, I'd like you to go upstairs and write down all the reasons why we get so worried and concerned when you're late. Could you do that for us, now, Sweetheart? And then we'll talk about it tomorrow.
Daughter:	OK, Dad.

Mom: Steve?

Son: What?

Mom: Do you have a few minutes to talk?

Son: I'm going to listen to my new tape right now.

Mom: Well, when would you be free for us to talk?

Son: OK, what do you want?

Mom: We seem to have a real problem settling things about your room.

Son: You know, you bug me about this all the time.

Mom: Yeah, I know. It's really gotten to be a sore issue for both of us, hasn't it!

Son: Yeah, I don't know why you don't just leave me alone. I mean it's *my* room!

Mom: It seems like a big part of the problem is the way we've been talking to each other. I guess you feel it's your room, and I should just butt out!

Son: Well, I haven't been hassling *you* about it!

Mom: Well I feel hassled too, especially when I find myself rooting around your room to get your dirty clothes for washing. I was hoping you might have some suggestions so we could get together and end the hassling.

Son: Why can't we just agree that it's my room, and that there's no reason for anybody to go in there or look at it.

Mom: You'd like your room to be 100% off limits to everyone but you? Can you think what would happen if no one but you ever went into your room?

Son: I think that would be just fine with me!

Mom: Well, you know I've been taking responsibility for picking up your clothes, washing them, and putting them back away.

Son: Well, I guess I could get a hamper in my room and maybe put my dirty clothes in there.

Mom: Gee, sounds good so far! But how would the clothes get to the washing area and back to the room after they're washed?

Son: Well you've always taken care of that!

Mom: Right, and that's where the hassle began, with me in your room. You were mad because I was in there, and I was upset because when I was in there I felt like a maid. I've decided not to do that anymore.

Son: Well, I don't know. Let's see. Maybe I could take the clothes downstairs and then bring them up after they're washed. Especially, if that would mean that you would keep out of my room.

Mom: Great! Now let me make sure we both understand our agreement. I will stay out of the room, and I'll wash only the clothes you bring downstairs. You'll have more privacy, and you'll also take responsibility for taking your clothes downstairs and carrying them back to your room after they're washed. Is that right?

Son: Yeah, that's it.

PASSIVE, AGGRESSIVE, AND ASSERTIVE PROBLEM-SOLVING APPROACHES

This session will offer you an opportunity to distinguish among **passive, aggressive,** and **assertive** problem-solving approaches in family matters.

When it comes to solving problems, each family member has his or her own way of doing things. **Awareness** of how each family member approaches problems is important for developing effective family problem solving.

You will have a chance to **discuss** and give **specific** examples of passive, aggressive, and assertive approaches to solving family problems, using specific **scenes from typical parent-adolescent interactions.**

NOTES
Related to Session 5

Form 8. Three Problem-Solving Styles

DIRECTIONS

1. Write what the following three words mean in terms of problem solving. That is, how would a "passive" person respond to a problem which came up in a family? How would an "aggressive" person respond? How would an "assertive" person respond?
2. Work together as a family in writing your answers.

PROBLEM-SOLVING STYLES

Passive: _____

_____

_____

_____

_____

_____

_____

_____

Aggressive: _____

_____

_____

_____

_____

_____

_____

_____

Assertive: _____

_____

_____

_____

_____

_____

_____

_____

Form 9. Problem-Solving Scripts: Parent Response Sheet

DIRECTIONS

1. The following five quotes are from adolescents.
2. Write typical "quotes" which a passive, aggressive, or assertive parent might make in response to each adolescent's quote.
3. Be sure to write three responses for each of the five adolescent quotes.
4. Each person is to complete this sheet by himself or herself.

QUOTES AND RESPONSES

"I'll pick whatever friends I want to."

Passive response: _____

_____

_____

Aggressive response: _____

_____

_____

Assertive response: _____

_____

_____

"The other kids don't have a curfew."

Passive response: _____

_____

_____

Aggressive response: _____

_____

_____

Assertive response: _____

_____

_____

(Continued)

"It's my room and I can leave it messy if I want to."

Passive response: _____

_____

_____

Aggressive response: _____

_____

_____

Assertive response: _____

_____

_____

"Why do I have to be treated like a kid? Why do you have to know where I'll be tonight?"

Passive response: _____ _____

_____

_____

Aggressive response: _____

_____

_____

Assertive response: _____

_____

_____

"All the kids smoke pot."

Passive response: _____

_____

_____

Aggressive response: _____

_____

_____

Assertive response: _____

_____

_____

Form 10. Problem-Solving Scripts: Adolescent Response Sheet

DIRECTIONS

1. The following five quotes are from parents.
2. Write typical "quotes" which a passive, aggressive, or assertive adolescent might make in response to each parent's quote.
3. Be sure to write three responses for each of the five parent quotes.
4. Each person is to complete this sheet by himself or herself.

QUOTES AND RESPONSES

"I don't want you hanging around those kids anymore."

Passive response: _____

_____

_____

Aggressive response: _____

_____

_____

Assertive response: _____

_____

_____

"You have to be in by 9:30 p.m. on weekdays."

Passive response: _____

_____

_____

Aggressive response: _____

_____

_____

Assertive response: _____

_____

_____

(Continued)

"Clean up your room."

Passive response: _____

_____

_____

Aggressive response: _____

_____

_____

Assertive response: _____

_____

_____

"Where are you going and who will you be with?"

Passive response: _____

_____

_____

Aggressive response: _____

_____

_____

Assertive response: _____

_____

_____

"No dope, and that's final."

Passive response: _____

_____

_____

Aggressive response: _____

_____

_____

Assertive response: _____

_____

_____

EXPRESSING FEELINGS CONCERNING FAMILY ISSUES

This session will give you an opportunity to practice specific **techniques** for effective communication, allowing each of you to **"get your point across"** while discussing **family** issues.

You will learn **verbal** and **nonverbal** communication **techniques.** You also will practice the art of **listening** which is essential to good communication.

NOTES
Related to Session 6

Form 11. Major Areas of Effective Communication

For effective communication, pay attention to three major areas.

      1. **WHAT** you say

      2. **HOW** you say it

      3. How well you **LISTEN**

1. ***WHAT*** you say

    a. Make sure you stay on the topic.

    b. Make sure you are specific and clear.

2. ***HOW*** you say it—Watch your nonverbal communication techniques.

    a. Eye Contact: Make sure you are looking at the person to whom you are speaking.

    b. Tone of Voice: Make sure you are not using a threatening, sarcastic, lecturing, whining, too loud, or too soft tone.

    c. Posture: Make sure your body communicates interest and concern (lean towards the person), rather than boredom (yawning, slouching, hands supporting chin, etc.), defensiveness (arms folded against your body), or aggression (finger-pointing).

3. How well you ***LISTEN***

    a. Make sure you can repeat what the other person has said.

    b. Check yourself on the nonverbal techniques listed above.

Form 12. Scoring Grid for Effective Communication on Family Topics

DIRECTIONS

1. Recognize that Forms 12 and 13 are to be used together.

2. Work as a family—parents and adolescent—in doing this activity.

3. Listen to directions from the leader as to how to perform this activity.

4. On the "Scoring Grid" (Form 12) on the first line under the speaker column place the adolescent's name. Under the listener column place the parent's name.

5. The speaker is to use the first listed "Family Topic," Form 13.

6. Speaker responds to topic listed on sheet with at least two sentences.

7. Listener is to repeat what speaker says.

8. The scorer is to grade (1 = good, 2 = very good, and 3 = excellent) the listener and the speaker on eye contact, tone of voice, posture, and content (i.e., did the speaker stay on topic and did the listener repeat what the speaker said without getting defensive?).

9. After completing Steps 6, 7, and 8, the scorer is to explain why the particular numbers were given for the speaker and for the listener.

10. Everyone is to take turns at being the speaker, listener, and scorer. Each person answers every topic on the list. However, this activity centers around parent-adolescent communication. Thus, the adolescent does not score mom and dad as speaker and listener with each other. Mom and dad are always either a speaker or a listener with the adolescent.

11. If only one parent and the adolescent of a given family are present for this activity, the speaker grades the listener and vice versa.

(Continued)

SCORING GRID FOR EFFECTIVE COMMUNICATION ON FAMILY TOPICS

List Name of Speaker	Areas to Score				List Name of Listener	Areas to Score			
	Eye Contact	Tone of Voice	Posture	Content		Eye Contact	Tone of Voice	Posture	Content

Score: **1 = Good** (has the general idea, but needs lots of practice)
          2 = Very Good (doing well, but still needs some practice)
          3 = Excellent (no problems!)

Form 13. Family topics for an Effective Communication Activity*

1. If I could change my family to make it better, I would . . .

2. The most patient member of my family is _____,
   who showed patience when _____.

3. If I had to describe my father in three words, I would say . . .

4. If I had to describe my mother in three words, I would say. . .

5. The one family activity that I really enjoy doing is . . .

6. The thing we disagree the most about in our family is . . .

7. When I know that I have upset someone in my family, I feel . . .

8. The time that I really had fun with my family was when . . .

9. I would describe an "ideal" family as . . .

10. A fantastic vacation for me and my family would be . . .

11. I show my love for the people in my family when I . . .

12. When I express anger, the members of my family react by . . .

13. The most generous member of my family is _____,
    who was generous when _____.

14. The most helpful member of my family is _____,
    who was helpful when _____.

15. The family member with the best sense of humor is _____,
    who showed that humor when _____.

16. If our family inherited a million dollars, I would like for us to _____.

17. Something I really need from my family is _____.

18. If I had to draw a picture of something to symbolize the members of my family, I
    would draw _____ for each member.

19. When it comes to the "rules" in my family, I feel . . .

20. The nicest thing that anyone in my family has done for me is . . .

*Adapted by Darrell J. Burnett, Ph.D., with permission from the *Ungame*® Company, 1975.

EXPRESSING POSITIVE FEELINGS TOWARD FAMILY MEMBERS

This session allows you to continue practicing the **techniques** you learned from the previous session, while you practice expressing **positive feelings** toward each other.

Giving and **receiving compliments** is an essential part of a healthy family communication pattern, especially when an adolescent is in the family!

During this session **no negatives are allowed!** Remember to use "I" statements, and to **stay positive!**

NOTES
Related to Session 7

Form 14. Scoring Grid for Effective Communication of Positive Feelings

DIRECTIONS

1. Recognize that Forms 14 and 15 are to be used together.

2. Work as a family—parents and adolescent—in doing this activity.

3. Listen to directions from the leader as to how to perform this activity.

4. On the "Scoring Grid" (Form 14) on the first line under the speaker column place the adolescent's name. Under the listener column place the parent's name.

5. The speaker is to use Form 15, "Stem Statements of Positive Feelings . . ."

6. Speaker responds to topic listed on sheet with at least two sentences.

7. Listener is to repeat what speaker says.

8. The scorer is to grade (1 = good, 2 = very good, and 3 = excellent) the listener and the speaker on eye contact, tone of voice, posture, and content (i.e., did the speaker stay on topic and did the listener repeat what the speaker said without getting defensive?).

9. After completing Steps 6, 7, and 8, the scorer is to explain why the particular numbers were given for the speaker and for the listener.

10. Everyone is to take turns at being the speaker, listener, and scorer. Each person answers every topic on the list. However, this activity centers around parent-adolescent communication. Thus, the adolescent does not score mom and dad as speaker and listener with each other. Mom and dad are always either a speaker or a listener with the adolescent.

11. If only one parent and the adolescent of a given family are present for this activity, the speaker grades the listener and vice versa.

(Continued)

SCORING GRID FOR EFFECTIVE COMMUNICATION OF POSITIVE FEELINGS

List Name of Speaker	Areas to Score				List Name of Listener	Areas to Score			
	Eye Contact	Tone of Voice	Posture	Content		Eye Contact	Tone of Voice	Posture	Content

Score: **1 = Good** (has the general idea, but needs lots of practice)
2 = Very Good (doing well, but still needs some practice)
3 = Excellent (no problems!)

Form 15. Stem Statements of Positive Feelings for an Effective Communication Activity

1. I am proud of you because . . .

2. The three things I like most about you are . . .

3. I felt closest to you when . . .

4. The three best times I ever had with you were when . . .

5. Your greatest talent is . . .

6. I really appreciated the time when you . . .

7. If I could grant you any three wishes, they would be . . .

8. You showed you really cared about me that time when you . . .

9. The three most pleasant memories of our family life are . . .

10. If I had to say something positive about each family member, I would say . . .

11. The thing I like best about home is . . .

12. The positive quality that you add to our family is . . .

EXPRESSING NEGATIVE FEELINGS TOWARD FAMILY MEMBERS

This session allows you to discuss **negative** issues with each other while continuing to use the **techniques** of effective communication.

The key to this session is to remain **civil, calm,** and **open** to what you hear.

Many families avoid negative discussions until they get to the yelling and screaming stage. This session will help you understand **how negative feelings arise** and how to deal with them **early** and **effectively.**

Just as healthy families give and receive compliments, it is also essential that families have an atmosphere where members feel **free to express negative feelings,** as long as they do so **appropriately.**

NOTES
Related to Session 8

Form 16. Scoring Grid for Effective Communication of Negative Feelings

DIRECTIONS

1. Recognize that Forms 16 and 17 are to be used together.

2. Work as a family—parents and adolescent—in doing this activity.

3. Listen to directions from the leader as to how to perform this activity.

4. On the "Scoring Grid" (Form 16) on the first line under the speaker column place the adolescent's name. Under the listener column place the parent's name.

5. The speaker is to use Form 17, "Stem Statements of Negative Feelings."

6. Speaker responds to topic listed on sheet with at least two sentences.

7. Listener is to repeat what speaker says.

8. The scorer is to grade (1= good, 2 = very good, and 3 = excellent) the listener and the speaker on eye contact, tone of voice, posture, and content (i.e., did the speaker stay on topic and did the listener repeat what the speaker said without getting defensive?).

9. After completing Steps 6, 7, and 8, the scorer is to explain why the particular numbers were given for the speaker and for the listener.

10. Everyone is to take turns at being the speaker, listener, and scorer. Each person answers every topic on the list. However, this activity centers around parent-adolescent communication. Thus, the adolescent does not score mom and dad as speaker and listener with each other. Mom and dad are always either a speaker or a listener with the adolescent.

11. If only one parent and the adolescent of a given family are present for this activity, the speaker grades the listener and vice versa.

(Continued)

SCORING GRID FOR EFFECTIVE COMMUNICATION OF NEGATIVE FEELINGS

List Name of Speaker	Areas to Score				List Name of Listener	Areas to Score			
	Eye Contact	Tone of Voice	Posture	Content		Eye Contact	Tone of Voice	Posture	Content

Score: **1 = Good** (has the general idea, but needs lots of practice)
2 = Very Good (doing well, but still needs some practice)
3 = Excellent (no problems!)

Form 17. Stem Statements of Negative Feelings for Effective Communication Activity

1. I get irritated when you _____

   _____

2. I get annoyed when you _____

   _____

3. I resent it when you _____

   _____

4. I felt embarrassed when you _____

   _____

5. I feel uncomfortable around you when _____

   _____

6. I felt hurt when you _____

   _____

7. I was disappointed when you _____

   _____

8. I felt angry towards you when _____

   _____

9. I feel that you didn't respect me when you _____

   _____

10. I have difficulty communicating with you when you _____

    _____

EXPRESSING FEELINGS OF EMPATHY TOWARD FAMILY MEMBERS

This session offers you an opportunity to practice your effective communication techniques while doing something that is difficult yet essential to healthy family communication.

You will practice how to *"get into each other's shoes,"* trying to understand and appreciate each other's thoughts, feelings, and opinions in areas common to families with adolescents.

This activity in **empathy** is very important, and will appear again in Session 15 during the family contracting activity.

NOTES
Related to Session 9

Form 18. Parent Sheet for Activities on Empathy Related to Family Issues

DIRECTIONS

1. Mom and dad are to work separately in completing this form while their teenager completes Form 19.

2. Mom and dad are to distinguish how each feels.

3. Recognize that Part A of this form addresses feelings of your teenager in connection with basic family issues which usually arise in the course of adolescence.

4. Recognize that Part B of this form addresses your feelings as a parent.

5. Complete both Part A and Part B.

6. Try to "get into each other's shoes," that is in Part A try to respond **as if you were your son or daughter.**

7. If you do not know in Part A what your teenager feels or thinks, guess; write what you would speculate he/she would feel or think.

8. Record your responses in the spaces provided.

_____   (Continued)

Form 18 Continued

Part A: Your Teenager's Feelings

DIRECTIONS

Write what your **son/daughter** might **think/feel** when facing peer pressure in the following areas. Mom and Dad answer separately.

PEER PRESSURE

1. He/she is at a party, and his/her friends encourage him/her to drink alcohol.

   Mom _____

   Dad _____

2. He/she is at a party, and his/her friends encourage him/her to use drugs besides alcohol.

   Mom _____

   Dad _____

3. He/she is at a party and his/her friends encourage him/her to stay out past curfew.

   Mom _____

   Dad _____

4. His/her friends want him/her to skip school after lunch.

   Mom _____

   Dad _____

5. He/she is faced with getting into or staying in a car with a drunk driver friend.

   Mom _____

   Dad _____

6. He/she is pressured by friends to have a party at his/her house while parents are out of town.

   Mom _____

   Dad _____

(Continued)

Form 18 Continued

7. He/she is pressured to hang around "friends" not approved by his/her parents.

   Mom _____

   Dad _____

8. He/she is pressured to wear clothes (hairstyle, make-up, jewelry) not approved of by his/her parents.

   Mom _____

   Dad _____

9. He/she is pressured to have sex.

   Mom _____

   Dad _____

Part B: Your Feelings as a Parent

DIRECTIONS

Write the things **you** might think or feel which would make it **difficult** for you to deal with the following situations.

SITUATIONS FACED

1. Your son/daughter asks to go out on his/her first unchaperoned date.

   Mom _____

   Dad _____

2. You son/daughter asks to get a driver's license.

   Mom _____

   Dad _____

3. Your son/daughter asks to drive the family car.

   Mom _____

   Dad _____

4. Your son/daughter asks you to stay out of his/her room.

   Mom _____

   Dad _____

(Continued)

5. Your son/daughter asks to go to a party at someone's house whom you don't know.

   Mom _____

   Dad _____

6. Your son/daughter asks you to extend his/her curfew from 10pm to midnight.

   Mom _____

   Dad _____

7. Your son/daughter seldom brings home books from school, claiming that he/she did his/her homework at school, or that the teachers never give homework.

   Mom _____

   Dad _____

8. Your son/daughter refuses to wear anything except "name label" clothes.

   Mom _____

   Dad _____

9. You find out that one of your son/daughter's friends is using drugs.

   Mom _____

   Dad _____

Form 19. Adolescent Sheet for Activities on Empathy Related to Family Issues

DIRECTIONS

1. Work independently in completing this form.

2. Recognize that Part A of this form addresses feelings of your parents—mom and dad.

3. Recognize that Part B of this form addresses your feelings as a teenager.

4. Complete both Part A and Part B.

5. In Part A, respond for mom on each issue and do the same for dad.

6. Try to **"get into each other's shoes,"** that is in Part A try to respond **as if you were Dad or Mom.**

7. If you do not know in part A what your mom or dad feels or thinks, guess; write what you would speculate he/she would feel or think.

8. Record your responses in the space provided.

(Continued)

Form 19 Continued

Part A: Your Parents' Feelings

DIRECTIONS

1. Write the things your **parents** might **think or feel** which would make it **difficult** for them to deal with the following situations.

2. Distinguish how Mom and Dad feel separately on each issue.

ISSUES

1. You ask your parents to go out on your first unchaperoned date.

    Mom _____

    Dad _____

2. You ask to get a driver's license.

    Mom _____

    Dad _____

3. You ask your parents for the family car.

    Mom _____

    Dad _____

4. You ask your parents to stay out of your room.

    Mom _____

    Dad _____

5. You ask to go to a party at someone's house whom your parents don't know.

    Mom _____

    Dad _____

6. You ask your parents to extend your curfew from 10 pm to midnight.

    Mom _____

    Dad _____

(Continued)

7. You seldom bring books home from school and you tell your parents that the teachers never give homework, or that you did your homework at school.

   Mom _____

   Dad _____

8. You tell your parents that you won't wear anything but "name label" clothes.

   Mom _____

   Dad _____

9. Your parents find out that one of your friends is using drugs.

   Mom _____

   Dad _____

Part B: Your Feelings as a Teenager

DIRECTIONS

Write things **you** might **think or feel** which would make it **difficult** when facing peer pressure in the following areas.

PEER PRESSURE

1. You're at a party and your friends encourage you to drink alcohol.

   _____

2. You're at a party and your friends encourage you to use drugs besides alcohol.

   _____

3. You're at a party and your friends encourage you to stay out past curfew.

   _____

4. Your friends want you to skip school after lunch.

   _____

5. Your friend is drinking and driving and you have to decide whether to get in the car, or, if already in the car, whether to stay in the car.

   _____

(Continued)

Form 19 Continued

6. Your friends are pressuring you to have a party at your house while your parents are out of town.

    _____

7. Your parents don't approve of certain friends of yours, but those friends are pressuring you to hang around them.

    _____

8. Your friends are encouraging you to wear clothes (hairstyle, make-up, jewelry) not approved of by your parents.

    _____

9. Your friends are talking about having sex and encouraging you to do likewise.

    _____

Form 20. Scoring Grid for Effective Communication of Empathy

DIRECTIONS

1. Recognize that Forms 18 and 19 are to be used together with this form.

2. Work as a family—parents and adolescent—in doing this activity.

3. Listen to directions from the leader as to how to perform this activity.

4. On the "Scoring Grid" (Form 20) on the first line under the **speaker** column place one of the parent's name. Under the **listener** column place the adolescent's name. The activity proceeds as follows.

5. The parent, as **speaker,** uses the first item on Form 18, Part A, and attempts to empathize, to "get into the adolescent's shoes." Using the response written for the "peer pressure" item, wherein the adolescent is at a party and friends encourage him/her to drink alcohol, the parent expresses what he/she thinks the adolescent might think or feel when facing peer pressure. Remarks are addressed directly to the adolescent.

6. As the **listener,** the adolescent simply **repeats back** what the parent said, thus showing that he/she was listening.

7. The other parent (if both parents are present), scores both the parent and the adolescent on Form 20, the "Scoring Grid," noting eye contact, tone of voice, etc., as in Sessions 6, 7, and 8. If only one parent is present, then the speaker (parent) and listener (adolescent) score each other.

8. The adolescent then becomes the **speaker,** staying on the same topic, explaining to the parent (listener) that, indeed, the parent was correct about the adolescent's feelings or thoughts. If the parent omitted certain thoughts or feelings which the adolescent had, then the adolescent communicates them to his/her parent.

9. The parent (listener) simply repeats back what was said.

10. Scoring again takes place on Form 20, "Scoring Grid" as was done in Direction 7.

11. The adolescent then becomes the speaker while attempting to empathize with his/her parent on the first item on Form 19, Part A (i.e., dealing with the first unchaperoned date). The adolescent attempts to "get into his/her parent's shoes" concerning the thoughts or feelings which might make it difficult for his/her parents to deal with the situation. Remarks are addressed directly to the parent.

12. The parent (listener) simply **repeats** what the adolescent said.

13. Speaker and listener are scored on Form 20, "Scoring Grid," as in Direction 7.

14. The parent then becomes the **speaker,** staying on the same topic, explaining that, indeed, the adolescent was correct about the parent's feelings or thoughts. However, if the adolescent omitted any feelings or thoughts which the parent had, or might have, this is communicated to the adolescent.

(Continued)

15. The adolescent (listener) simply **repeats** what the parent said.

16. Parent and adolescent are scored on Form 20, "Scoring Grid," as in Direction 7.

17. This procedure is continued, using each item on the empathy sheets (Forms 18 and 19), until all items have been discussed (if time permits).

18. Throughout this activity, participants are reminded to remain calm and stay on track.

(Continued)

Form 20. Continued

SCORING GRID FOR EFFECTIVE COMMUNICATION OF EMPATHY

List Name of Speaker	Areas to Score				List Name of Listener	Areas to Score			
	Eye Contact	Tone of Voice	Posture	Content		Eye Contact	Tone of Voice	Posture	Content

Score: **1 = Good** (has the general idea, but needs lots of practice)
2 = Very Good (doing well, but still needs some practice)
3 = Excellent (no problems!)

Form 21. Parent Sheet for Activity on Empathy Related to Hospital Issues

Part A: Your Teenager's Feelings

DIRECTIONS

Write the things your **son/daughter** might have thought or felt or probably would think or feel when facing the following situations.

SITUATIONS FOR PART A

1. When my adolescent was informed about being admitted to the hospital, he/she thought/felt

   _____

2. During the admission procedures, my adolescent thought/felt

   _____

3. When we said goodbye and left the hospital on the day of admission, my adolescent thought/felt

   _____

4. During our visit when our adolescent was having a "good day," he/she thought/felt

   _____

5. During our visit when our adolescent was having a "bad day," he/she thought/felt

   _____

6. On the first off-grounds pass with family, our adolescent thought/felt

   _____

7. On the weekend family pass, our adolescent thought/felt

   _____

8. As we developed our home behavior contract during family sessions, our adolescent thought/felt

   _____

9. As we anticipate discharge from the hospital, our adolescent thinks/feels

   _____

(Continued)

Form 21 Continued

Part B: Your Feelings as a Parent

DIRECTIONS

Write the things *you* have thought or felt or probably would think or feel when facing the following situations.

SITUATIONS FOR PART B

1. When I had to make the decision to hospitalize my adolescent, I was thinking/feeling

   _____

2. When I admitted my adolescent, I was thinking/feeling

   _____

3. When I left the hospital after admitting my adolescent, I thought/felt

   _____

4. When I visited my adolescent and he/she was having a "good day," I thought/felt

   _____

5. When I visited my adolescent and he/she was having a "bad day," I thought/felt

   _____

6. When I picked up my adolescent for his/her first off-grounds family pass, I thought/felt.

   _____

7. When my adolescent came on his/her weekend passes, I thought/felt

   _____

8. As we developed our home behavior contract during family sessions, I thought/felt

   _____

9. As we anticipate discharge from the hospital, I am thinking/feeling

   _____

Form 22. Adolescent Sheet for Activity on Empathy Related to Hospital Issues

Part A: Your Parents' Feelings

DIRECTIONS

Write those things your parents thought or felt or probably would think or feel when faced with the following situations.

SITUATIONS FOR PART A

1. While my parents were attempting to make the decision concerning whether to hospitalize me or not, they thought/felt

   _____

2. During admission procedures, my parents thought/felt

   _____

3. After admission procedures were completed, and my parents were leaving the hospital, they thought/felt

   _____

4. During visits with my parents on days when I was having a "good day," they were thinking/feeling

   _____

5. During family visits with my parents on days in which I was having a "bad day," they were thinking/feeling

   _____

6. When I went on my first off-grounds pass, my parents were thinking/feeling

   _____

7. When I went on my weekend off-grounds pass, my parents were thinking/feeling

   _____

8. While we were developing the home behavior contract during family session, my parents were thinking/feeling

   _____

9. As we anticipate discharge from the hospital, my parents are thinking/feeling

   _____

(Continued)

Form 22 Continued

Part B: Your Feelings as a Teenager

DIRECTIONS

Write those things you thought or felt or probably would think or feel if facing the following situations.

SITUATIONS FOR PART B

1. When I was informed that my parents had decided to hospitalize me for treatment, I thought/felt

   _____

2. During the hospital admission procedures, I thought/felt

   _____

3. When my parents left the hospital after the admission procedures were completed, I thought/felt

   _____

4. During family visits on days when I was having a "good day," I thought/felt

   _____

5. During family visits on days when I was having a "bad day," I thought/felt

   _____

6. During the first off-grounds pass with family, I thought/felt

   _____

7. During the weekend family pass, I thought/felt

   _____

8. While developing the home behavior contract during family session, I thought/felt

   _____

9. As we anticipate discharge from the hospital, I am thinking/feeling

   _____

Part III

RECOGNIZING
BEHAVIOR
AS A
FUNCTION
OF ITS
CONSEQUENCE

THE LAW
OF EFFECT

Beginning with this session, the topic will center around trying to **understand** human behavior and the **principles of behavior change.**

This session will involve a discussion of the LAW OF EFFECT, which states that behavior is a **function** of its **consequence.** That is, if you want to know **why** a behavior **keeps going,** or **stops,** then look at the **consequence.** Look at what happens after the behavior occurs.

Starting with this session, you will be discussing **behaviors** and **consequences** and how they help explain why we act the way we do.

The more you understand about how behaviors happen, the more you will understand the "how" and "why" of each family member's behavior.

NOTES
Related to Session 10

Form 23. The Law Of Effect: Behavior Is A Function Of Its Consequence

INFORMATION

1. A problem behavior is tied in with the adolescent's **perception** and **experience** of the **consequence** for the behavior.

2. If an adolescent **perceives** and **experiences** a consequence for behavior as **pleasant,** the behavior is likely to **increase.**

3. If an adolescent **perceives** and **experiences** a consequence for a behavior as **unpleasant,** the behavior is likely to **decrease.**

4. Most adolescents will eventually stop the behavior, based upon the consequences which the adolescent **perceives** and **experiences** as **unpleasant.** The spectrum of unpleasant consequences ranges from verbal warnings to prison!

5. The task of parents with adolescents is to communicate to them that there are **unpleasant** consequences for problem behaviors, and **pleasant** consequences for positive behaviors.

THE CONTINUUM OF UNPLEASANT CONSEQUENCES

Setting	Consequence (Listed in sequential order of experienced unpleasantness)
Home	Lecture, Restriction, Diversion Counseling, Probation
School	Lecture, Detention, Suspension, Expulsion, Diversion Counseling, Probation
Community	Lecture, Restitution, Diversion Counseling, Probation
Probation	Informal, Formal, At home, Group home, Camp, Youth Prison

THEORIES OF ADOLESCENT BEHAVIOR

This session offers an overview of **four theories** of why adolescents act the way they do.

You will hear about **analytic, humanistic, biological (developmental),** and **behavioral** explanations of adolescent behaviors.

A special discussion will be held on the importance of understanding the **developmental age** of each adolescent. Also a discussion will occur of how some biological, developmental **delays** in the **central nervous system** can help account for certain adolescent behaviors.

In addition, a discussion will take place about how to **identify** possible "problem areas" in development, and how to use **specific learning techniques** to work on these problem areas at **home.**

NOTES
Related to Session 11

Form 24. Sample Profile of an Acting-out Adolescent

DIFFICULTY OBSERVED	EMOTIONAL CORRELATES
Sequencing Deficits	Low Tolerance of Frustration
	Impulsivity
Verbal Expression Deficits	Explosiveness
Social Judgment Deficits	Egocentricity
	"All or None" Syndrome

Form 25. Treating the Deficit

Characteristics and Emotional Correlates to be Treated	Treatment Procedure

Sequencing Deficits	Classroom activities:
	    Active listening
	    Reading exercises
	        (Drawing conclusions)
	
	Home Behavior Contract:
	    "Earn" privileges.
	    Reward for appropriate behaviors.

Low Tolerance of Frustration	Promote self-control.
Impulsivity	Self management techniques
Explosiveness	Relaxation
	Biofeedback
	"Earn" privileges.
Verbal Expression Deficits	Home communication exercises (See Sessions 6, 7, 8, and 9)
Social Judgment Deficits	Social skills training
	Empathy exercises (See Session 9)

PARENTAL ROLE
IN APPLYING
CONSEQUENCES

This session centers around the topic of ***consequences,*** and the role which parents play in ***applying*** consequences for their adolescent's behaviors at home.

This session will involve a discussion of 5 basic steps for parents to use in attempting to raise responsible adolescents, who can handle the consequences of their own actions.

As the steps are discussed by way of cartoon illustrations, you will have an opportunity to discuss with each other how well these steps have been used in your family.

You will also have an opportunity to plan for future implementation of the steps with each other.

NOTES
Related to Session 12

**Form 26. Five Basic Steps for Parents to Help Adolescents
Associate Consequences With Behaviors**

RAISING RESPONSIBLE KIDS:
FIVE BASIC STEPS

1. BE CONSISTENT

2. SAY WHAT YOU MEAN
   MEAN WHAT YOU SAY

3. DON'T RESCUE

4. DON'T GIVE IN

5. LOOK FOR THE POSITIVES

Cartoon 1. BE CONSISTENT

Form 27. Examples of Inconsistency Experienced Within the Family

DIRECTIONS

1. Mom and dad work together on this task.
2. Each adolescent works independently.
3. Write examples of inconsistency experienced within the family, i.e., between parents, between one parent and one adolescent, one parent saying or doing one thing with the adolescent and the other parent doing differently.
4. Place the emphasis upon finding examples of inconsistency, not upon faultfinding.
5. Keep your comments for use later in Session 12.

Mom's and Dad's Examples

_____

_____

_____

_____

_____

_____

_____

Adolescent's Examples

_____

_____

_____

_____

_____

_____

_____

_____

Cartoon 2. SAY WHAT YOU MEAN—MEAN WHAT YOU SAY

"I THOUGHT YOU ALREADY *TOLD* ME FOR THE LAST TIME TO EAT MY CARROTS!"

Cartoon 3. DON'T RESCUE

MARVIN

Form 28. Examples of Rescuing or Being Rescued

DIRECTIONS

1. Mom and dad work together on this task.
2. Each adolescent works independently.
3. Parents are to write incidents where they remember "rescuing" their child.
4. Adolescents are to write memories of times when they were "caught" by their parents, but, for one reason or another, they were "let off the hook."

Mom's and Dad's Examples

_____

_____

_____

_____

_____

_____

_____

_____

_____

Adolescent's Examples

_____

_____

_____

_____

_____

_____

_____

_____

_____

_____

Cartoon 4. DON'T GIVE IN

Reprinted with special permission of Mell Lazarus and Creator Syndicate

Reprinted with special permission of King Features Syndicate, Inc.

Cartoon 5. LOOK FOR THE POSITIVES

ANDY CAPP By Reggie Smythe

Reprinted with special permission of North America Syndicate, Inc.

Form 29.   86 Ways to Say "Very Good"*

1. Good for you!
2. Superb.
3. You did that very well.
4. You've got it made.
5. Terrific!
6. That's not bad!
7. Couldn't have done it better myself.
8. Marvelous!
9. You're doing fine.
10. You're really improving.
11. You're on the right track now!
12. Now you've figured it out.
13. Outstanding!
14. That's coming along nicely.
15. I knew you could do it.
16. Good work.
17. You figured that out fast.
18. I think you've got it now.
19. I'm proud of the way you worked today.
20. Tremendous!
21. You certainly did well today.
22. Perfect!
23. Nice going.
24. You've got your brain in gear today.
25. Now you've got the hang of it.
26. WOW!
27. Wonderful!
28. You're getting better every day.
29. You're learning fast.
30. You make it look easy.
31. That's a good boy/girl.
32. That's very much better.
33. Super!
34. You did a lot of work today!
35. Keep it up!
36. You've got that down pat.
37. Congratulations.
38. Exactly right!
39. Nice going.
40. Excellent!
41. Sensational!
42. You're doing beautifully.
43. You've just about mastered that!
44. That's really nice.
45. That's the best ever.
46. That's great.
47. Way to go!
48. That's the way to do it!
49. That's quite an improvement.
50. Good thinking.
51. You're really going to town.
52. Keep up the good work.
53. That's it!
54. That's better.
55. You haven't missed a thing.
56. Fantastic!
57. You outdid yourself today!
58. You're doing a good job.
59. That's the right way to do it.
60. That's better.
61. Right on!
62. Well, look at you go!
63. That's the best you've ever done.
64. That's RIGHT!
65. You must have been practicing!
66. Great!
67. Keep working on it, you're getting better.
68. You remembered!
69. That kind of work makes me very happy.
70. You're really working hard today.
71. That's what I call a fine job!
72. I knew you could do it!
73. I'm very proud of you.
74. One more time and you'll have it.
75. Fine!
76. That's good.
77. Good job.
78. You really make this fun.
79. Good remembering.
80. Nothing can stop you now.
81. You are doing much better today.
82. Keep on trying.
83. You are really learning a lot.
84. You've just about got it.
85. I've never seen anyone do it better.
86. You are very good at that.

*Reprinted with permission. Growing Parent. January, 1985. Vol. 13, #1.

PUNISHMENT VERSUS LOGICAL AND NATURAL CONSEQUENCES

This session discusses the difficult task of **how to apply negative consequences for negative behaviors** in the family.

You will learn to distinguish between **PUNISHMENT** versus the application of **LOGICAL AND NATURAL CONSEQUENCES.**

You will have an opportunity to **assess** just how **negative** consequences have been **applied** in **your family.**

You will also have an opportunity to **assess** how **positive** consequences have been **applied in your family.**

Finally, you will have an opportunity to discuss present and potential **resources** at home for offering consequences for behaviors.

NOTES
Related to Session 13

Form 30. How Parents Deliver Negative Consequences*

DIRECTIONS

1. Mom and dad work separately on this task.
2. Each adolescent works independently.
3. Parents rate themselves.
4. Adolescents rate their parents.
5. Below is a list of five statements concerning how **negative** consequences are delivered at home. Simply check yes or no as to whether they apply to how mom or dad deliver negative consequences.

STATEMENTS	Mom		Dad	
	Yes	No	Yes	No
1. The consequence is a retaliation to get even or humiliate.	___	___	___	___
2. The consequence is logically understandable and reasonable to the child.	___	___	___	___
3. The consequence is given in a calm voice and/or with empathy and concern for the child.	___	___	___	___
4. Consequences are arbitrarily imposed for the purpose of inflicting pain or suffering.	___	___	___	___
5. The intensity of the consequence is appropriate to the behavior.	___	___	___	___

---

*Adapted by Darrell J. Burnett, Ph.D., from Jensen, L., and Jensen, J., *Four Principles for Positive Parenting.* Brigham Young University. Provo, Utah. 84601. 1984.

Form 31. How Parents Deliver Positive Consequences*

DIRECTIONS

1. Mom and dad work separately on this task.
2. Each adolescent works independently.
3. Parents rate themselves.
4. Adolescents rate their parents.
5. Below is a list of five statements concerning how positive consequences are delivered at home. Simply check yes or no as to whether they apply to how mom or dad delivers positive consequences.

STATEMENTS	Mom		Dad	
	Yes	**No**	**Yes**	**No**
1. I have rewards that mean a lot to my child.	____	____	____	____
2. I clearly state just what behaviors I expect.	____	____	____	____
3. I start with small enough steps to make it easy for my child to meet my expectations.	____	____	____	____
4. I am enthusiastic when I present rewards.	____	____	____	____
5. I am willing to follow through with rewards even when other important demands are placed on me.	____	____	____	____

*Adapted by Darrell J. Burnett, Ph.D., from Jensen, L., and Jensen, J. *Four Principles for Positive Parenting.* Brigham Young University, Provo, Utah 84601. 1984

Form 32. Parental Resources For Consequences *

DIRECTIONS

1. Mom and dad work together on this task.
2. Each adolescent works independently.
3. Parents identify items which they are **presently** using as consequences.
4. Adolescent identifies items being used by parents as consequences.
5. Below is a list of items which other families have used as positive consequences for positive behaviors. They have also been withdrawn and used as negative consequences for negative behaviors. Simply check each item which is **presently** being used by mom or dad as a consequence.

ITEMS FOR CONSEQUENCES

HOME	Mom	Dad	ACTIVITIES	Mom	Dad
Meals	___	___	Extra-curricular activities	___	___
Use of T.V.	___	___	Summer vacations	___	___
Use of musical equipment	___	___	Free time at home after school	___	___
Use of rooms	___	___	Saturdays	___	___
Books	___	___	Family games	___	___
Furniture	___	___			
Invitation for friend to visit	___	___			
Parties (Birthday, sleepovers, etc.)	___	___			
Room decorations	___	___	SOCIAL/EMOTIONAL		
Toys	___	___	Affection	___	___
Clothing	___	___	Company of siblings	___	___
			Attention	___	___
OUTSIDE THE HOME HELP			Time together	___	___
Transportation	___	___	Compliments	___	___
Money	___	___	Games and sporting events	___	___
Finding jobs	___	___	Visiting and conversation	___	___
Enrolling in recreational activity	___	___	Listening to problem of child	___	___
Enrolling in lessons	___	___	Helping solve problems of child	___	___
Signing for auto purchase	___	___			
Insurance	___	___			
Trips	___	___			
Help getting along: siblings	___	___			
Help getting along: teachers	___	___	YOUR PERSONAL HELP		
Help getting along: adults	___	___	Help on homework	___	___
Help getting along: peers	___	___	Help on cleaning	___	___
Help getting along: relatives	___	___	Transportation to activities	___	___
			Answering questions	___	___
POSSESSIONS					
Use of car	___	___			
Use of computer	___	___			
Use of stereo and video	___	___			
Use of phone	___	___			
Discount tickets	___	___			
Games and Sporting Events	___	___			

*Adapted by Darrell J. Burnett, Ph.D., from Jensen, L., and Jensen, J. *Four Principles for Positive Parenting.* Brigham Young University. Provo, Utah 84601. 1984.

IDENTIFYING BEHAVIORS

While the previous two sessions dealt with the topic of **consequences** for behaviors, this session dwells on the importance of being specific when it comes to the **behaviors** expected of each other in families.

You will have an opportunity to get **specific** while discussing "vague" words which seem to come up a lot in family discussions: TRUST, RESPECT, UNDERSTANDING, AND RESPONSIBLE.

This session will help you prepare for the next session, on **contracting,** where you will learn to connect behaviors with consequences.

**NOTES
Related to Session 14**

Form 33. Defining Behaviors Worksheet

DIRECTIONS

1. Write your definition for each of the following four words.
2. Do not discuss at this time with any other group member. Work alone.

Trust

_____

_____

_____

_____

Respect

_____

_____

_____

_____

Understanding

_____

_____

_____

_____

Responsible

_____

_____

_____

_____

_____

DEVELOPING A FAMILY BEHAVIOR CONTRACT

This session will give you an opportunity to practice how to **negotiate** and **contract** with each other in an effort to promote **positive** behaviors toward each other.

You will practice a **"seven (7) step"** sample *family contract activity* to give you a "feel" for using this approach to promote **positive problem solving** in the family.

NOTES
Related to Session 15

Form 34. Family Behavior Contracting*

PURPOSE: Increase positive interactions.

    1. Be specific.
    2. Be realistic.
    3. Have **empathy,** "get into the other person's shoes."

ACTIVITY	**Seven (7) Steps**
1. Pick 3 items on your list from Form 35 or 36.	(1. Identifying rewards for **others)**
2. Pick 2 items on other person's list from Form 35 or 36.	(2. Identif)ying rewards for **self**
3. Rank other person's list according to what you value (V) the most. Use 1 to 5 with 1 being most valued.	(3. Setting **priorities** on rewards)
4. Rank your list according to what will be the most difficult, what will cost (C) the most. Use 1 to 5 with 1 being most.	(4. Setting **costs** on providing rewards)
5. Review both lists to see if all items are realistic and specific.	(5. Making sure items are **realistic** and **specific)**
6. Empathize. Try to "get into the other person's shoes" as you review the values and costs on each item (i.e., adolescent tries to relate why he/she thinks a specific item is difficult for parent to do).	(6. **Empathizing)**
7. Negotiation. Bargain with each other (between parents and adolescent), offering positive behaviors to each other.	(7. **Trading off** rewards)

*Adapted by Darrell J. Burnett, Ph.D., from Weathers, L. and Liberman, R.P., The Family Contracting Exercise. *Journal of Behavior Therapy and Experimental Therapy.* 1975, 6, 208-214.

Form 35. Parent Catalog Cards: Reinforcers for Teens

DIRECTIONS

1. As parents of a given family, work together as a team on this activity.
2. Note that the eleven (11) items listed are ones that other families have in the past listed as possible behavior areas which could be used as rewards for their teenage children.
3. Choose three (3) items, no more and no less, which you believe your adolescent would most appreciate.
4. Use space 12 to write in any item or items not listed.
5. Work as a team to arrive at a common estimate of reward items which you believe your adolescent would like the most.
6. Disregard the letters "V" and "C" until instructed later on how to use them.
7. After completing Directions 1 through 6, follow additional directions given by the group leader.

REINFORCERS FOR TEENS

1. Stop nagging your adolescent about _____

   _____

   V _____   C _____

2. Let your son/daughter stay out longer, until ___:___ on weekdays, and ___:___ on weekends

   _____

   _____

   V _____   C _____

3. Let your son/daughter go out another night per week. _____

   _____

   V _____   C _____

4. Give your adolescent _____ per week allowance _____

   _____

   V _____   C _____

5. Buy your adolescent a _____

   _____

   V _____   C _____

6. Let your adolescent watch TV more _____

   _____

   V _____   C _____

(Continued)

Form 35 Continued

7. Let your adolescent use the family car (to) _____

_____

V ____   C ____

8. Stop going through your adolescent's things _____

_____

V ____   C ____

9. Stop listening in on your adolescent's phone calls _____

_____

V ____   C ____

10. Stop being critical of your adolescent's clothes, hair, friends, etc. _____

_____

V ____   C ____

11. Let your adolescent get a driver's license. _____

_____

V ____   C ____

12. _____

_____

_____

_____

V ____   C ____

Adapted by Darrell J. Burnett, Ph.D., from Weathers, L. and Liberman, R.P., The Family Contracting Exercise. *Journal of Behavior Therapy and Experimental Therapy.* 1975, 6, 208-214.

Form 36. Teen Catalog Cards: Reinforcers for Parents

DIRECTIONS

1. As adolescents, work independently on this activity.
2. Note that the 16 items listed are ones that other teenagers in the past have listed as possible behaviors that could be used as rewards offered to their parents.
3. Choose three (3) items, no more and no less, which you believe your parents would most appreciate.
4. Use space 17 to write in any item or items not listed.
5. Be specific in writing each of your items.
6. Disregard the letters "V" and "C" until instructed later on how to use them.
7. After completing Directions 1 through 6 follow additional directions given by the group leader.

REINFORCERS FOR PARENTS

1. Do ____ minutes of homework nightly—from ___:___ to ___:___ _____

_____

                           V ____   C ____

2. Make my bed and hang up my clothes before I go to school _____

_____

                           V ____   C ____

3. Clean my room, which means _____

_____

                           V ____   C ____

4. Not talking back or arguing when _____

_____

                           V ____   C ____

5. Bring my friends to meet my parents. Friends are _____

_____

                           V ____   C ____

6. Improve my grades in the following:

    Class _____ To _____

    Class _____ To _____

    Class _____ To _____

                           V ____   C ____

_____   (Continued)

7. Attend ____ classes at school every day with less than ____ tardies per _____

_____

                                                       V ____   C ____

8. Not run away from home _____

_____

                                                       V ____   C ____

9. Not smoking (at) _____

_____

                                                       V ____   C ____

10. Help with chores around the house such as: _____

_____

                                                       V ____   C ____

11. Ask parents' permission to go out _____

_____

                                                       V ____   C ____

12. Be home by ___:___ weekday nights and ___:___ weekend nights. _____

_____

                                                       V ____   C ____

13. Get up in the morning without a hassle, which means _____

_____

                                                       V ____   C ____

14. Babysit my younger brother/sister when _____

_____

                                                       V ____   C ____

15. Play my stereo/TV/radio more quietly when _____

_____

                                                       V ____   C ____

16. Not fight with my brother/sister when _____

_____

                                                       V ____   C ____

17. _____

_____

                                                       V ____   C ____

Adapted by Darrell J. Burnett, Ph.D., from Weathers, L. and Liberman, R.P., The Family Contracting Exercise. *Journal of Behavior Therapy and Experimental Therapy.* 1975, 6, 208-214.

BIBLIOGRAPHY

BIBLIOGRAPHY

Bean, R., and Clemes, H. (1980). *How to teach children responsibility.* Los Angeles, CA: Price, Stern, Sloan.

Becker, W. (1971). *Parents are teachers.* Champaign, IL: Research Press.

Brownstone, J., & Dye, C. (1973). *Communication workshop for parents of adolescents.* Champaign, IL: Research Press.

Burnett, D. (1982, Spring). The learning disabled delinquent: Teaching socially appropriate reactions to confrontations for negative behaviors. *Journal of Special Education Technology.* Volume V; No. 2, 44-52.

Burnett, D. (1991). *Parents, kids, and self esteem: 15 ways to help kids like themselves.* Audiotape. P.O. Box 7223, Laguna Niguel, Ca 92607-7223.

Burnett, D. (1991). *Raising responsible kids: 5 steps for parents.* Audiotape. P.O. Box 7223, Laguna Niguel, Ca 92607-7223.

Goldstein, A., Sprafkin, R., Gershaw, N., & Klein, P. (1980). *Skill-streaming the adolescent: A structured learning approach to teaching prosocial skills.* Champaign, IL: Research Press.

Growing Parent, (1985, January) Vol. 13, No. 1. Lafayette, IN 47902: Dunn and Hargitt, Inc. 22 N. Second Street.

Jensen, L., & Jensen, J. (1984). *Four principles for positive parenting.* Provo, UT: Brigham Young University.

Weathers, L., & Liberman, R.P. (1975). The family contracting exercise. *Journal of Behavior Therapy and Experimental Therapy.* 6, 208-214.

The *Ungame* Company. (1975). Anaheim, CA 92806: Post Office Box 6382.

ABOUT
THE
AUTHOR

ABOUT THE AUTHOR

Dr. Darrell Burnett, father of two teens and a pre-teen, is licensed as a clinical psychologist and as a marriage, family, and child counselor. He is credentialed as a community college teacher and counselor, and as a high school teacher and school psychologist.

He earned his Ph.D. in clinical psychology from United States International University in San Diego, California.

Following his one year Post Doctoral Fellowship in psychology at the Neuropsychiatric Institute, UCLA, Dr. Burnett has maintained an active private practice for more than 15 years in southern California working with troubled youth and families, developing programs for emotionally disturbed youth. Using his experience as a former drug counselor for the Federal Narcotic Addict Rehabilitation Program, he also develops treatment programs for chemically dependent youth.

Dr. Burnett presently consults with two psychiatric hospitals, following 12 years as Program Director of three hospital-based treatment units for youth, including a consultant contract to establish a hospital-based treatment program for youth at the naval base in Okinawa.

Dr. Burnett's contracts as a consultant include schools, probation departments, military bases, churches, social agencies, and business corporations.

Following 10 years as an Adjunct Professor at the Graduate School of Human Behavior, United States International University, Dr. Burnett maintains his academic interests through writing journal articles and presenting seminars and workshops on parent-child relationships, stress and anger management, teen suicide, and self esteem, at the local, state, national, and international levels.

He maintains media involvement through TV and radio presentations.

Dr. Burnett's avocation is promoting youth sports as a positive experience. He is the author of a series of booklets on positive coaching: *The Art of Being a Successful Youth League Manager-Coach* (Funagain Press, P.O. Box 7223, Laguna Niguel, CA 92607-7223).

Dr. Burnett is presently the Director of the Responsibility Center in Orange County, California.

He is listed in the National Register of Health Providers in Psychology. He is a member of the American Psychological Association and the California State Psychological Association.